I0056179

Show Up Like a Coach: It Will Change Your Life

Jennifer Gervès-Keen, MA, MCEC

Publisher's Note

Every possible effort has been made to ensure that the information contained in this book is accurate at the time of going to press, and the publishers and authors cannot accept responsibility for any errors or omissions, however caused. No responsibility for loss or damage occasioned to any person acting, or refraining from action, as a result of the material in this publication can be accepted by the editors, the publisher or the author.

First published in Canada by JGK Consulting in 2022
This edition published in the United Kingdom by Ideas for Leaders Publishing, a business of IEDP Ideas for Leaders Ltd, 2024.

Apart from any fair dealing for the purposes of research or private study, or criticism or review, as permitted under the Copyright, Design and Patents Act 1988, this publication may only be reproduced, stored or transmitted, in any form or by any means, with the prior permission in writing of the publishers. Enquiries concerning reproduction should be sent to the publishers at the following address:

Ideas for Leaders Publishing
42 Moray Place
Edinburgh
EH3 6BT
www.ideasforleaders.com
info@ideasforleaders.com

ISBN 978-1-915529-34-3

© JGK Consulting 2022

Table of Contents

To purchase copies of this book and other titles from this
series please visit www.ideasforleaders.com/our-book-store

or use this QR code

www.ingramcontent.com/pod-product-compliance
Lightning Source LLC
Chambersburg PA
CBHW050432240326
41458CB00130BA/6472

Why Coaching Matters

Coaching is seeing others for who they truly are and then helping them get where they want to be. It's basic, elemental human connection that creates safe spaces where people can be vulnerable and share their biggest dreams and all the fears that run alongside them. It's asking questions to help identify their destination, then providing a GPS to allow them to get there. I often say that my role as a professional coach is to change the gears and nudge the steering wheel when needed, and maybe check the GPS from time to time. My clients are the ones doing all the driving.

This book is a how-to guide for professionals who need to effectively communicate with others in their organization – so, essentially, everyone in the workforce today. Corporate leaders will certainly find the core skills outlined in this book critical to their success. These tools are universal. They can be used by everyone in almost every situation, whether it's having to give your favourite team member difficult feedback at work or it's sitting down and really listening to your 14-year-old son at home.

Our world is more connected than ever before, yet, paradoxically, people are feeling more disconnected. Learning the basic tools of coaching and how to use them is essentially learning how to rewire your brain to communicate. Understanding coaching skills will not only make you more effective as an organizational leader, it will also make you more effective at managing your life in general.

A few years ago, I had a client who was a senior leader in a professional services firm. Let's call him Marc. I had been working with Marc for about six months when I ran into Elaine, one of his team leaders. Elaine and the team knew Marc was working with a coach. Elaine admitted she had been on the verge of quitting about four months earlier. Marc's behaviour as a leader had prompted her to second-guess her own competency and her place in the organization. Through Marc's interactions with Elaine's team – who quickly learned they could run to him whenever they weren't happy with one of Elaine's decisions – Marc was constantly undermining her leadership. As with many leaders, Marc's

Unfortunately,
our understanding seems
to be light years ahead
of our actual behaviour,
and that's what needs
to change.

behaviour came from a good place. Though he was genuinely trying to help the members of Elaine's team who kept showing up in his office, he was also simultaneously disregarding the effect of his behaviour on his team leads, who were feeling undermined and unsupported.

Elaine had decided to give it another month while she looked for a new position. This was the same month Marc started integrating his new coaching and self-awareness skills into his day-to-day interactions. Thanks to Marc's efforts, Elaine decided to give him another chance and ultimately ended up staying with the team. She was thrilled that she could stay in a job she loved with a leader who was not only becoming more effective in his role, he was also infinitely more open to receiving feedback from his team.

Moments like these, when I see my clients effecting positive change in themselves and others, are the moments where the power of coaching truly comes into its own. We are finally starting to understand that if we focus on people first, the rest (retention, productivity, service levels, profit, impact, etc.) will follow.

Unfortunately, our understanding seems to be light years ahead of our actual behaviour, and that's what needs to change.

I am passionate – and often get on my soapbox – about teaching leaders how to coach, because I believe this will ultimately make our organizations healthier, which will, in turn, directly improve the quality of people's lives. Though I certainly can't solve the many issues our planet is facing today, I do firmly believe that if people were able to have better experiences at work, they would take that positive energy home with them and possibly do something wonderful with it – and that is within my power to achieve.

Positive energy can come to life as a direct result of positive interactions with others. Creating deep and honest connections with others takes time and effort, and it is more than worth the investment. Deep connections don't have to be personal. You don't, as a business leader, need to know every single minor detail about each of your employees. You *do* need to be able to build trust and create a conversational space where they feel they can easily approach you to let you know

I do firmly believe that if people were able to have better experiences at work, they would take that positive energy home with them and possibly do something wonderful with it.

what's going on in their lives when these issues may affect how they show up on the job.

This book will provide you with a toolbox of essential coaching tools, such as listening intently, communicating effectively and being endlessly curious. It will also discuss the mindset of coaching (a generous, non-judgmental way of seeing the world and not being afraid to speak the truth) and why even though people understand and appreciate this approach intellectually, they are often incapable of actually carrying it out.

Our organizations struggle to set individuals up for success. Much of that responsibility falls on our leaders. There is so much going on in any given organization – the pressure to keep up with changing economics, increasing customer demands, ever-changing norms, desires of employees, changing values and constant ambiguity – it can bog leaders down. Making the time to focus on the person in front of you is challenging, yet it is the only way to move people and organizations forward in a truly sustainable manner.

Making the time
to focus on the person
in front of you is
challenging, yet it is
the only way to move
people and organizations
forward in a truly
sustainable manner.

I grew up living in a series of small mining towns across Canada (with a brief foray into Greenland). My dad was a highly respected mining engineer who specialized in northern and arctic mining. At the time, I thought a specialization in warm weather mining might have been a more reasonable choice. In hindsight, I am immensely grateful for the unique experiences my parents created for me. Why is my upbringing relevant to this book, you ask? Because it helped to instill in me a lifelong fascination with people, patterns, and the psychology of groups and organizations. It was an enlightening experience early on in my career to realize that people working in a remote arctic mining camp could have similar challenges to people working in an international law office in Paris. It gave me the mindset of an explorer – curious, questioning and continuously looking for the next destination. It also taught me the importance of seeing opportunities, even (and maybe especially) during times of adversity. Finally, it gave me what I call pragmatic empathy – always willing and able to be generous with others in understanding their perspective, unless that perspective becomes a barrier to their growth (which is when the pragmatic side of my empathy surfaces).

I have spent the past 15 years coaching and training organizational leaders, and close to 30 years working with and leading people. I specialize in leadership and executive coaching and, specifically, in helping leaders understand how to be *better* leaders (and people) by weaving coaching into their basic communication skills.

When people ask me how I found coaching, I always tell them that coaching found me – and stuck. By nature, I am an insatiably curious person, eternally fascinated by people and their stories and always seeking to learn more about those around me. I also possess an uncanny ability to detect patterns and connect the dots regarding people's behaviour. Being a coach allows me to help leaders truly understand their impact on others and how it creates a ripple effect on both their organizations and the personal lives of their employees.

Like many people, I didn't always know what I wanted to be growing up. I started my career on the administrative side of politics, where I learned a great deal about communication and how not to behave. Knowing instinctively that I needed something more, I quit my job, sold everything I owned and flipped a coin to decide between my two favourite cities: Paris and Barcelona. Paris won! I started life from zero in Paris (speaking only rudimentary high-school French), with no job, no friends and no place to live.

After several years of migrating from managing law offices to press and public relations, I started my own training company and worked with global companies, training their leaders how to communicate, negotiate and conduct business in English. Fast-forward 13 years. I've owned my own business on the west coast of Canada for the past 10 years and have built a reputation as a frank, practical coach, who is open to challenging and supporting people to see things from an entirely different perspective – with no judgment. I have worked in many types of organizations – from seniors' homes to financial institutions, engineering firms to casinos, airplane manufacturers to charitable foundations. The smallest organization I worked with had five employees; the largest over 200,000 worldwide. One of the best parts of my job is the diversity of the organizations I get to work with. The common element in all is the humanity.

According to many of my clients, I add "instantaneous value" as soon as I walk into the building. I am grateful for the success I have had and incredibly appreciative of the clients I have been privileged to work with over the past 10 years. They have inspired me to write this book.

Whether I'm speaking at a conference or in a room of 100-plus new leaders learning how to coach, I am constantly asked if I have additional resources to share – if there is something they can look up or buy to continue practising the core skills I've taught them. This book is that resource.

You
Too Can
Coach

Coaching, at its best, is a consistent mindset – a way of approaching the world with generosity, curiosity and empathy. It is a way of being. Becoming a better coach means practising the tools yourself first and then using them to coach others. It all comes down to *paying attention*.

What most people experience in coaching is the toolbox: a skillset – as opposed to a mindset – where you ask powerful questions, raise awareness around someone's behaviour and then help them achieve their goals. There are more and more people in organizations who are learning or practising the toolbox, and it is making a concrete, measurable difference. It's vital that we spend more time developing and encouraging the coach mindset.

While I truly believe that anyone can learn how to coach, developing the mindset of a coach poses a much bigger challenge. It requires real commitment and emotional labour, including the following three steps:

1. Do the work. By that, I don't mean take a course, get certified or complete hundreds of

Do the work.

hours of practice. I mean you need to work on *yourself.* To be an effective coach, you need to:

a. know who you are (that means being self-aware)

b. manage who you are when needed (it's hard to be generous if you can't manage your own biases)

c. be genuinely curious about the individual or team you are coaching

Though these steps may seem simple, they will be hard to achieve if you don't like yourself or haven't spent enough quality time with yourself to be truly comfortable with who you are. It's very difficult to sit in a place of generosity and empathy with others if you can't get there for yourself. So, do – the – work.

2. Practise presence continuously. Being 100% focused and aware of the person or team you are working with is one of the most valuable gifts you can give in coaching – and in life in general.

3. Embrace the opportunity to grow. This is
    where true resilience shines through. There
    is always something to learn, especially when
    things get tough. Much of my role as a coach
    is to help my clients reframe their difficult
    experiences so that they are able to get
    themselves unstuck.

Being 100% Present

Presence is powerful. It's a true gift – something that's rare and hard to come by in our world of constant vibrations, notifications and "thumbs up." Being fully present for someone else creates an energy between the two of you that allows an unexpected honesty to emerge. The connection deepens, the truth is spoken and you arrive at your destination so much faster.

Being fully present in your life (that is, *really* paying attention to your surroundings) changes everything. It is the difference between living your life on the sidelines and fully participating on the field. You don't have to change your entire lifestyle to accomplish this: you just need a little effort and self-discipline to see results.

Learn to create space for others. Show up 100%, and allow them to show up (in all their glory) with all their bumps and bruises. Presence is not about being perfect, it's about being there. It's simple, it's powerful and it's hard to do.

After coaching one of my clients, she expressed that the experience of having someone across from her who was 100% present, with no agenda or ego getting in the way, was invigorating. By being present – by fully seeing and hearing the person in front of you for who they are – you are giving that person a simple gift, yet one that has long-lasting repercussions.

It's impossible to be fully present without paying attention to yourself and to others. Look around you, notice what's happening, and pay attention to the small details. Be generous and curious, go beyond your own biases to entertain other points of view, and learn to view scenarios through other people's eyes. Be receptive to whatever shows up, honour it and then dance with it. Respect the good and the exciting right along with the bad and the mundane. Learn to identify your triggers, including the things, individuals, situations and emotions that derail you from being present and force you back into your own internal story. It's our own narratives that get in the way of being present, not anyone else's.

Being present means creating empathy around things that you may not fully understand or even agree with. To be empathetic, you must be able to put yourself in another person's shoes. This may not be so easy for coaches, because we haven't always experienced what our clients are going through. Being an empathetic coach is more about holding the space for someone and respecting a certain tension that is present between where that person is and where they want to be. As a coach, my job isn't necessarily to fully understand a client's situation or to dive in and resolve any tension present; it is to create an energy of empathy within the conversation so they can fully understand their own situation, how they got there and how they want to move forward. It is in stress, discomfort and tension where we most grow. We can't help someone explore these uncomfortable spaces without empathy or generosity. When we are not generous with our patience and time, we try to "fix" things quickly. We try to resolve the situation or find brilliant solutions, when often all the person needs is the time and the headspace in which to explore the tension present in their life. As a coach, this requires managing my own view of the world and what I think a client should do, because ultimately that doesn't matter. In the end, it's always about them, not me. Empathy is humanity at its best, so practise it generously and without limits.

Focus on the Journey

Joan flew into the meeting room red-faced and breathless. As usual, she was a few minutes late, no doubt coming from a previous meeting that ran-over. Her ever-present water bottle was glued to one hand, her cell phone to the other and her laptop somehow miraculously balanced in between. Joan, a senior leader in the public service in her late 50s, had been working for the government since she graduated university. Dedicated and earnest, she applied everything we talked about seriously. She always did her homework and felt incredibly guilty about *everything* – and I mean everything. Delving further into the topic of guilt would require an additional book, so I will simply say that it is often a worthless emotion. If guilt doesn't actually drive you to action, it will only serve as a huge drain on your emotions and energy, often proving to be downright destructive.

Joan's brain was amazing. Though she openly shared everything about her work, I knew practically nothing about her life outside of the office. All I learned was that she had a nice apartment in an expensive downtown neighbourhood, she was frantically working towards a secure and stable future, and she was on her own, with no other family depending on her.

It was time to discover how Joan felt about her impending retirement and see what she was doing to prepare for this monumental life change. So, we stopped working on her leadership skills and stopped talking about her team, her boss, and all the players on her stage at work. We started, instead, to really talk about Joan – her goals, her dreams and her future.

After two years of dancing around her fear of retiring, Joan had taken the difficult step of submitting her request for early retirement. It was probably one of the hardest and most important decisions of her life. Forever a planner, forever pushing her own emotions and thoughts down deep into herself and doing things because it was what was expected, I was curious to see how Joan would deal with the reality of no longer following a plan decided by someone else. As it turned out, not well.

Joan's retirement had always been a destination, never a journey. She had missed out on years' worth of opportunities to be present, to show up in her own life, to come down from the spectator bleachers and play, to relish in the small slivers of day-to-day joys, and to discover what really made her tick and propelled her emotions. Joan was driven to do only one thing: succeed. So, she went through life checking off points on a to-do list she didn't write; one that was never even truly hers.

Focused on a point of the map that others defined as "success," Joan never faltered and never once took her eye off that grand prize. The consequence of her ambition was that she completely missed living her life along the way to her so-called success. In her own words, "I

It's amazing how good we are at lying to ourselves until we actually sit down and give ourselves a straight-up chat.

have been working my entire life towards a box labelled 'retirement.' Now, I'm finally there, opening up the box, ready to live my life at last, only to find that the box is completely empty. I have no life. I can't see the future. I don't know what to do."

When you are not present in your own life, you can get so focused on the mirage ahead of you that you deliberately put blinders on to avoid seeing the detours along the way. Doing so frees you from the responsibility of having to make choices – which means never having to be wrong, never having to take risks and, most importantly, never having to fail. Just remember that choosing to stay safe in this manner can come at a great cost.

When you are not present for other people, you spend your time looking over their shoulder, searching for what's next, and looking out for something better and brighter. As a result, you completely miss out on living your life to the fullest.

Practising Presence: Helpful Tips

The following section outlines a few simple daily strategies to help you practise being more present. If you prefer using apps or more structured frameworks, Google "mindfulness activities" or "meditation apps." To work on becoming more present in a sustainable way, be sure to only focus on one small, incremental action at a time. Trying to accomplish too many of these tasks at once will overload your brain and hinder your ability to focus, thereby reducing your chance of success.

Being Present with Yourself

Find a favourite quote, a motivating phrase (e.g., "pay attention!") or a simple question (e.g., "What am I thinking / feeling / seeing / hearing right now?"), and program a

notification reminder on your phone /
computer / watch that randomly reminds
you a few times a day to stop and think.

Do a debrief with yourself when you get
derailed. Ask the following questions to help
identify your "distraction" triggers – the ones
that send you into judgmental, dismissive or
less generous behaviour:
- What happened?
- Up until what point was I present?
- When did I stop?
- Why did I stop?

Stop and smell the roses, literally and
figuratively. Quickly run through your
five senses. What am I seeing? Hearing?
Feeling? Smelling? Tasting? This helps to
immediately bring you in touch with your
current surroundings and notice the small
details around you.

Coach yourself. Usually, after an unexpected reaction triggered by something (or, more oftentimes, someone), I have an internal dialogue with myself (or you can talk to yourself out loud if it helps, although I wouldn't recommend doing it on public transit), and I ask myself, "Why am I so upset? What are the facts? What am I assuming? Can I understand the other person's point of view? Do I even want to?" It's amazing how good we are at lying to ourselves until we actually sit down and give ourselves a straight-up chat.

Breathe deeply. It will go a long way in helping you settle your mind to push past panic.

Being Present with Others

Take a look at yourself and your surroundings. Is your phone attached to your hand? If not, I bet it's somewhere close by and clearly visible, isn't it? Sorry, turning it over so you can't see the screen doesn't count. It's lurking there, a physical presence as sensitive as a ticking time bomb. Are there other physical barriers in the room (computers, laptops, tablets, etc.)? Any loud noise that will get in your way? Any interruptions you know will take place? If you are speaking on the phone, what would visually distract you, and what might the caller on the other line be able to hear that could distract them?

To be present with others, you must clear the decks. Firmly plant your feet on the ground. If you are speaking to someone face-to-face, remove your cell phone from view, give that person your full attention and be sure to make consistent eye contact. If you are speaking with someone over the phone, start the conversation by asking them where they are, as that will allow you to visualize their surroundings. Be sure to remove visual distractions if possible, and try your best to eliminate potential interruptions before they happen.

A 10-minute conversation with someone where you are 100% present is more valuable than an hour when you're only half there. Keep yourself on track, and try to apply the 70/30 formula. You should be listening 70% of the time and speaking only 30% of the time. Give them the floor, and don't check out. Lean in, be focused and be receptive. More importantly, don't feel you need to fix things. Trust that those communicating with you are competent. They will get there on their own, and they will feel good that they did. Listen to learn and not to judge, to solve the problem or to come up with a brilliant response. The difference is incredible, and people will feel it and truly appreciate it. In the end, you will walk away having learned more from others than you ever thought possible.

Being
Curious

Genuine curiosity with no agenda not only builds trust, it also allows you to move past biases and get out of operating from your own perception. Curiosity leads you to dig deeper. Things are often not as they seem. So, by proceeding with your initial superficial interpretation of someone's behaviour, you may miss out on finding the root cause of that behaviour.

Curiosity runs much deeper than just asking thought-provoking questions. Genuine curiosity helps us get past bias and judgment and leads us into the realm of empathy. It creates a space of trust that allows people to let down their guard and open up, perhaps even offering you key insights into their lives, all due to your genuine interest in knowing more about them.

Curiosity is a mindset. The older we get and the more experience we have, the more we need to regularly practise being curious. When we start feeling like we know everything there is to know about something, we lose that wide-eyed creative spark of the unqualified beginner. It is then that we need to fight the hardest to bring ourselves back to a curious state of mind.

Curiosity is a mindset.

Asking great questions forms a valuable tool in both coaching and developing curiosity. The following are guidelines outlining what makes for great questions:

1. Steer clear of "why" questions. Contrary to popular belief, the most effective questions in coaching conversations do not start with "why." A "why" question demands a reason, requires a justification and immediately imposes pressure, particularly in a one-on-one situation. For a little word, it packs a lot of punch and can cause people to shut down rather than open up. "Why" narrows a question down until people sometimes start hearing an accusation instead of a query. Using "what" and "how" in place of "why" broadens the situation and provides the individual with some breathing space and reflection time.

2. Keep your questions short. There is nothing worse than trying to figure out what is being asked in a long-winded, run-on question.

3. Don't put the answer you are hoping for into the question – that means *no leading*. Also, don't help the person by giving them options

a, b or c to choose from. That just motivates laziness, and, as a result, you will never get a genuine response. For example, if you start by asking, "What has you stressed?", do not continue by offering answers like, "Work? Home? New boss? Your presentation next week?" Trying to be "helpful" by offering up answers to your question won't allow the individual to dig deeper to find the *real* answer. Force people to think (especially in uncomfortable situations), as it is in those stressful scenarios where we can most grow.

4. Stop speaking as soon as you ask the question. Don't be tempted to fill any awkward silence that ensues. The other person *will* speak eventually. As a Certified Mentor Coach, I listen to numerous audio recordings of coaching conversations, many of them from the leaders I work with. The number one mistake they make is asking a great question, waiting only a millisecond and then quickly following it up with another question ... and another ... and then even offering multiple choice options or attempting to answer the

questions themselves. The key is to ask the question, then *zip it* until the other person speaks. If they don't have an answer to a worthy question, then that should be their homework to take away with them.

5. Ask genuine questions by posing them in your own language. If you Google "powerful coaching questions," you will find no shortage of questions to choose from. Just make sure to customize the questions to fit your personal language and leadership style. Be real. Find what works for you. Two of my personal favourite questions are "What's getting in your way?" and "Let's unpack that" (which technically isn't even a question, rather an invitation to dive deeper into the issue).

Dig Deeper
Before You Judge

John was a top performer and an exceptionally intelligent man with a great work ethic. I was asked to coach him because the leadership team was noticing behaviours that could indicate declining motivation (including ever-increasing conflict with his supervisor), and they were concerned he was preparing to leave the organization.

When I met with John's supervisor, I was actually shocked (and I am not easily shocked) by the amount of judgment and bias he held towards John. Convinced that John was being deliberately sloppy in his work and displaying a lack of concern that bordered on unprofessional, he showed me a pile of examples of John's work, which were full of grammatical errors that simply weren't up to standard. From what I knew of John, he was incredibly smart, well-spoken and a bit of a perfectionist with a healthy ego. The picture John's supervisor painted simply did not match the person I had perceived John to be.

When I asked John about the errors, there were both confusion and frustration in his response. We talked about whether he had ever had difficulty in school. Even though his oral communication was practically perfect, all the errors were showing up in his written reports and PowerPoint decks. After a few conversations and some extra digging to arrive at the root of the problem, John decided to go through a series of assessments to see if there was a disconnect he was missing. Turned out that what John thought he was writing and what was actually coming through on the page weren't the same – there was, indeed, a disconnect happening in his brain. To resolve this issue, John now uses voice recognition software and also has someone proofread his work. Today, John is successfully running his own organization.

Never assume you know what's behind someone's behaviour. Digging deeper to discover the root cause will increase the level of connection, understanding and empathy you have with that individual. If your interaction is with an employee or a team member, chances are their level of engagement will increase because you took the time to listen and be curious. Not simply accepting a situation at face value and choosing to dig deeper may take more time and require more effort, yet the lasting impact you create as a result will produce a positive, long-term ripple effect.

Practising Curiosity: Helpful Tips

Learn! The best way to keep your brain firing on all cylinders is to learn. If you're an online learner, you can benefit from all the Massive Open Online Courses (MOOCS) now available from providers such as Coursera or EdX. If you prefer to learn in person, check out local conferences, speakers, café discussions, debates or readings – the opportunities are endless.

Create a human library for yourself. Make a list of all the people you know and all the topics they might know. Then invest in buying them a coffee, and take the opportunity to ask them all the questions you can think of about their speciality.

If you're a reader, read. Read things you wouldn't normally read about subjects that may not initially interest you. If you're not a reader, then listen. There are many free audio resources available, including audio books, podcasts, interviews and radio stations.

Ask questions. Whether you're having a conversation with a team member or a discussion with your partner, ask questions. Practise turning a declaration like, "You should really..." into a question like, "What do you want to do?" I can tell you one thing:

the more you use questions instead of answers, statements or judgments with your own children, the greater the chance they will grow up to possess curious and questioning minds.

Create mantra questions. Find one or two questions that suit your communication style, and tag them to any appropriate conversation. For example, "What's getting in your way?" or "What's important to you about this?" As previously discussed, try to avoid starting questions with "why." Focus, instead, on the "what" and the "how." Keep the questions broad, and resist the urge to jump in and present people with the answer. Give people the time they need to come up with an answer all on their own.

Listen to learn. Ask for people's stories, not their resumes. Where are they from? Where did they grow up? What was their life like up until today? What do they care about? What's important to them? These types of questions will help you capture a person's true story.

Listening to Learn

Listening, much like empathy and curiosity, is another skill set which you can actually improve with practice. In both the workplace and at home, there are generally three obstacles that can stand between you and effective listening:

1. External distractions: We are constantly surrounded by distractions, including screens, noise, other things we'd rather be doing and other people we'd rather be talking to. Five-to-ten minutes of active and curious listening is more valuable and more impactful than an hour-long meeting where you are distracted. Save yourself time, and truly listen to the other person.

2. Internal distractions: Often times, our own thoughts, fears, doubts, biases and judgments are racing along much faster than the person who is talking to us. It takes effort to shut down those invisible distractions and move from an internal focus to an external one.

3. Ego, positive intent or a combination of the two: When a person tells us about a problem or difficult situation, we generally want to help. We may even find ourselves having

Five-to-ten minutes
of active and curious
listening is more valuable
and more impactful than
an hour-long meeting
where you are distracted.

solved the problem in our head long before the person has finished speaking. So, we wait impatiently for our chance to jump in and impress them with our brilliant idea. When you do this in a coaching conversation, the conversation then becomes all about you, not about the person you are coaching.

Listening and its dance partner *presence* make the difference between a conversation where someone walks away feeling seen and heard (regardless of whether or not their issues were resolved) or walks away feeling small and frustrated. Ask yourself what kind of impact you want to make.

Sometimes there is value in interrupting. I know that goes against what we were all taught by our parents and teachers growing up, so it can be a very hard thing to do. When someone is stuck in their story, especially if it's a narrative you have heard before, it can be incredibly powerful to just hold your hand up and say "What's important to you about this?" or "What do you want to do about this right now?" Chronic rants are not helpful. The more we tell our own stories out loud and to ourselves, the more we believe them and the more they become our truth. You must listen with intent to hear what's behind the story.

Listening to learn allows you to pick up what's not being said – to hear between the lines. It also helps you to hear habits – certain phrases that people turn to time and time again to help themselves explain, and sometimes justify, their behaviours. These habits can become a permanent part of a person's story over time. I have had more than a few clients who unknowingly set themselves up for sabotage by the very language they used.

You can listen just as effectively over the phone as you can in person. Just be mindful to find your focus, concentrate on the voice coming from the other end, and pay attention to the highs and lows in their tone and energy. Many people are uncomfortable with coaching over the phone because they feel they lose the visual advantage, especially when it comes to reading body language. Phone coaching is just as effective, sometimes more so, than in-person coaching. If you have an individual who is more reserved and you are having difficulty drawing them out of their shell, coaching them over the phone often provides a safety barrier, as it allows them to feel less vulnerable. The more comfortable they feel, the more likely they are to share more of themselves. It is also important to always be very deliberate in your questions and your observations. Phone coaching can ultimately make you a better in-person coach.

It Will Get Better When

Like many busy people, Ali was very fond of the phrase "It will get better when ..." As in "It will get better when we get this project done," "It will get better when the new person comes on board," "It will get better when I come back from vacation." The reality is, when you start working from vacation to vacation or thinking that the new hire will magically solve all your problems, you will veer off track. These are temporary band-aids that don't actually fix anything.

"It will get better when ..." became Ali's mantra – something he repeated to himself so often, he didn't even realize he was saying it. It became an excuse that allowed him to avoid taking action, doing real work or changing his own behaviour. As a result, Ali avoided saying "no" to the things he didn't want and failed to focus his attention on the things he really wanted. Solely depending on external events to fix your life will get you absolutely nowhere.

Being a good listener will help you hear others' verbal "tics" as well as your own, so you can put them under the coaching microscope and figure out what they are a symptom of. There are people who spend their whole lives muttering the same things over and over, and we don't call them on it. It becomes a shield and, in their eyes, a valid excuse until it gets so embedded in their reality they can no longer find their way out from under its shadow. If too much time passes, they often grow so comfortable in its presence that they may not even want to get out. Finding reasons not to change is *so* much easier than effecting change can ever be.

Practising Listening: Helpful Tips

Give yourself a goal. Whether it's heading into a meeting or a coaching session, task yourself with one or two specific things you want to notice or be aware of.

Work on being present, and your listening skills will automatically improve. If you find yourself mentally drifting, bring yourself back and ask the person speaking to "rewind." Chances are they will be more succinct the second time around and may even learn something through the repetition. If you miss information, don't pretend you were listening. Not only is that disrespectful to the person speaking, it can also lead you to uncertain territory, as you may have missed vital information to the conversation you are continuing to have. Honestly admitting that you lost the conversational thread for a few seconds is the best and simplest solution. This will give the speaker the chance to reframe and repeat the story in a way that may prove to be more articulate and more direct to ensure that you understand them.

Be intentional in choosing your environment. Whenever you can, set yourself up for success. Be wary of noise barriers, physical barriers, and visual and auditory distractions. Learn what works for you, and be deliberate and transparent about making it happen.

Listen to learn, not to respond. This is the most important element of being an effective listener. Try to listen to someone without jumping in to solve their problem or perhaps without even speaking. Just focus on watching the person's body language, studying their facial expressions and gauging their energy. If you are communicating over the phone, focus on the person's voice and tone. Whenever you can, be an observer and hone your radar. You will be amazed at how much detail you can pick up when you are paying attention.

The Grey of Empathy

There is a lot of talk about empathy, and our general lack of it, in today's world. While people may confuse empathy with sympathy, they are vastly different. Sympathy elicits feelings of pity for a person, while empathy requires much more than that – it requires genuine understanding.

Having empathy does not mean agreeing with someone or making them feel good. It's about listening to learn their story, it's about understanding their point of view, and (most importantly) it's about taking the time and energy to trace their path and find a way to relate to it. In the end, we are all in some way products of our environments. Putting your own views aside and allowing someone else's experiences to take precedence in your mind is how true empathy is created.

Today, we are in desperate need of more *real* empathy in this world (not the fake politically correct projections that we seem to be getting so good at portraying). While empathy is difficult to achieve, it is well worth the effort. It helps invite tough conversations where people feel comfortable to express what they really think

Nothing will change in our organizations or our personal lives until we start communicating with empathetic honesty. This requires bravery, courage, integrity and a lot of energy.

and how they really feel, knowing the other parties are listening to learn and understand rather than judge. Empathy also requires resisting the urge to pose solutions and quick fixes to people's problems. We are often driven to quickly fix the problem and move on, as that allows us to avoid difficult and potentially complex emotions. The quicker we solve the problem, the better we can feel about ourselves. Yet, by doing so, we miss the opportunity to reflect and learn from our own reactions and judgments.

Nothing will change in our organizations or our personal lives until we start communicating with empathetic honesty. This requires bravery, courage, integrity and a lot of energy. Sometimes, I wonder if the world is just too tired to practise consistent empathy. There is no doubt that it's much easier and more comfortable to categorize people into boxes with familiar labels. Doing so helps us easily make sense of things. It's comfortable, it's safe and it just feels right. True empathy is uncomfortable, murky and sometimes even painful, as it forces us to re-examine ourselves and our own beliefs in an attempt to step outside of them and into another person's. In the end, we are all flawed beings. It's time we learned to forgive ourselves, as well as others, and use these flaws to connect with one another in an honest way.

The fears of falling short, of not being good enough and of being judged close us off from others, which makes empathy for others very difficult to practise. Yet it is through our flaws that we connect to each other as human beings. While perfection is bright, shiny and beautiful, it is also rigid, impenetrable and virtually impossible to connect with.

In my entire coaching career, I can count on one hand the times I refused to work with someone because I felt that they were "uncoachable" at that particular point in time. Individuals I've found to be uncoachable, though intelligent and ambitious, have possessed the lethal cocktail of narcissism, lack of self-awareness and lack of empathy. When mixed together, these qualities turn any person into Teflon – nothing sticks. I consider the fact that I have worked with hundreds of leaders over the years and only encountered a few of these profiles to be highly promising for the human race as a whole.

Everyone has a chink in their armour. To practise empathy, look for those possible entrances (those passages to light), and view them not as weaknesses to use in exploiting the person, rather as starting points on which to build common ground. This is an important cornerstone to the foundation of any real relationship.

Find Your Common Ground

Joe was a manager in a unionized environment that had suffered a toxic senior leader for the previous three years. We were on the long, long road of turning the organization's culture around. Joe, once considered to be one of the more engaged and progressive leaders on the team, had understandably checked out. After three years of dealing with a leader who led using fear, who publicly shamed the entire management team and who constantly rejected his ideas, Joe had given up and gone into survival mode.

We were a team of four coaches tasked with working with a management team of 14 leaders. Each leader met with us individually to choose the coach they wanted to work with through a process that roughly resembled speed dating, spending seven minutes with each coach to assess compatibility. Joe didn't want to choose a coach, because he didn't have any trust in the process. He was entrenched in survival mode, perceiving any change (negative or positive) as a threat. His external shell was as hard as an armadillo's, and he had zero interest in the "fluffy stuff" as he bluntly told me during our first meeting. In the end, I was the coach who worked with Joe, and I was eager to take on the challenge despite the fact that several people in his organization expressed their "sympathy" for me.

Joe was described to me as grumpy, tough, cynical and someone who would be impossible to coach. This only increased my curiosity about him. In my experience, individuals who come with that much perceived baggage almost always have the most interesting stories to tell.

Understanding that Joe's resistance was high, I didn't try to persuade him of the benefits of coaching or of the changes we were going to make to the organizational culture. I simply asked about him – how long he had worked in the organization, what role he started in, what motivated him to apply for a management role, and how he felt at that moment about what was happening. If you ask people how they feel generally, they will find this a very difficult question to answer because they often don't know exactly how they feel. If you ask them to give you a word to describe the mood they are in *right now*, you will always get an answer, and it will often be an illuminating one. When trying to connect with a person through curiosity and empathy, it's important not to get drawn into their negativity. Simply accept that negativity as a natural part of their story, and move on.

I also delved into Joe's life outside of the organization. We talked about how he spent his time out of the office. I learned that he had a son, had been married for over 25 years and was passionate about martial arts, even teaching classes on weekends for the past several years. He read everything he could get his hands on about how the brain and body worked together in order to use that information in his martial arts classes. That was my way into the chink in his armour.

I made Joe a deal. I promised I would share with him everything I knew about neuroscience if he accepted to meet with me regularly so we could slowly build up the trust necessary to pierce through his external concrete layer. This was obviously taking a bit of a risk. In general, you don't make "deals" with those you coach, because you want to work with individuals who are receptive to what you have to offer them, not people you have to coerce into meeting with you.

It took a couple of months to get to a place where Joe felt comfortable enough to share his experiences at work. It took a few more months for him to get to a place where he started holding himself accountable for how he was showing up on the job. Though it wasn't easy, he did get there.

He was a challenging client who really pushed and pulled every step of the way. He had no patience for things like team-building exercises or leadership retreats, as he thought they were all a waste of time. So I really had to rein in my natural positivity and optimism, because I knew that would lead him to shut down. He was a fascinating and complex human being, and it was a true privilege to work with him. We kept in touch until his retirement a few years later.

When a person gives you permission to work your way into the chinks in their armour, they are trusting you with the enormous responsibility of taking care of them in a way that works for them. That means that you respect *their* needs, *their* worldview and *their* goals, and that you work with them using *their* communication style. Without genuine empathy, you may inadvertently squander that precious opportunity. If you lose a person's trust after working so hard to gain it, not only will you likely never gain it back, you will also lose the richness of having that relationship in your life.

Practising Empathy: Helpful Tips

Ask people to tell you their story. By that, I don't mean their professional story (we can all recite our resumes), I mean their *real* story. Where did they grow up? How many siblings do they have? What was their favourite subject in school? What was one thing they learned as a kid that they still use as a leader today? Having insight into a person can really help us change the lens through which we see them, and that will ultimately impact how we relate to and interact with them.

Make people right in your mind. When you just can't see eye to eye with someone, step outside your own mindset and try seeing their perspective as the right one (at least in your head). The only black and white that exists in the world is in science and math. Human behaviours, thoughts and emotions are all various shades of grey. They are not concrete – just purely based on our memories, beliefs and worldviews. Spend more time swimming in the grey, and you will start to understand the motivation behind other people's behaviour. While you don't have to agree with everyone, you do have to be willing to understand the path they traveled to arrive at their point of view.

Ask more questions. Use curiosity to get you out of a state of judgment and into a state of wonderment. You'll quickly realize that wonderment is an amazing state of mind where things are alive with possibility. It's a joyful space entirely devoid of cynicism and sarcasm. It keeps your brain vibrantly young and eternally curious — kind of like putting yourself in the mind of a five-year-old who's still discovering the world.

Be okay with not knowing the answer. Our natural desire to fix a problem and appear that we know our stuff can completely obliterate any opportunities to practise empathy. Just focus on seeking to understand the person's situation. Don't offer a solution or even try to make them feel better, just be present.

Hear What You Are Saying

Language is the fundamental element of how we communicate with one another. Our body language, chosen words and delivery tone team up to make a powerful package, especially when you add in clear intent and deliberation. In a world where our egos are as fragile as eggshells, it is easy to be hurt by words, which can wound like weapons (whether intentionally or unintentionally). Add to that any given organization's complexity and jargon, along with a diverse and multi-cultural, multi-lingual workforce, and it's a wonder we manage to succeed in communicating at all.

Be purposeful in your language. Watch for habits, tics, expressions, biases and judgments that can alter what you are trying to express. Though words are triggers to our emotions, most of us don't listen carefully enough to decipher the intent behind someone's words. Instead, we tend to take their words at face value to save both time and effort.

Webster's Dictionary, the leading reference of the English language, has always taken great joy in announcing the latest "new" words that are

Incorporating "but" into a sentence allows us to avoid being direct and yet say potentially damaging things to people without taking on any ownership.

added every year. I'd like to offer some suggestions of words they should consider removing – starting with the word "but."

Incorporating "but" into a sentence allows us to avoid being direct and yet say potentially damaging things to people without taking on any ownership. I personally think we could easily get along in life without the word. It only serves to negate the words that come before it and often sets people up for failure in feedback conversations, as it tends to convey mixed messages. Take the following feedback sentence, for example, "Susan, I really loved the work you did on the report, but you need to pay more attention to the details." Well, did you really like her work, or does she need to pay more attention to the details? Most people will choose either one of those statements to believe. The person will either falsely believe they did a great job or focus solely on the negative and feel discouraged. The word "but" is also the ideal vehicle for passive aggressive "niceness," a behavioural illness that has affected society at large. Case in point, take the expression "no offence, but ..." It's clear that you will give offence with that statement, so at least have the guts to own the fact that you are about to insult someone.

Let's take a sentence like, "You've been doing fairly well so far, but..." What a wasted opportunity to give clear, concise feedback to someone. If a change is desired, directly communicate this. If it's a behaviour that is potentially going to get a person fired one day, tell them *now*. We are often so afraid of being unpopular or disliked that we phrase our feedback, feelings, comments and observations in such vague platitudes that they are left completely open to interpretation. Then we wonder why people don't implement our feedback as we intended. We defend our vague method of communicating by telling ourselves that by being less direct (less harsh, if you will), we are sparing people's feelings. The truth is we are avoiding taking responsibility for our own.

Practise being clear in your messages. Use short sentences, and try to avoid the word "but" at all costs – that includes the word "however" (which is just a fancier "but"). Use facts when describing a situation and not your own judgment

The truth often does not offend, it's the judgment layered into the truth that hurts people.

or interpretation. Be brave enough to speak the truth. The truth often does not offend, it's the judgment layered into the truth that hurts people.

If we look at language through a leadership lens, we'll notice that a lot of what we define as "executive presence" comes back to the words we use. Executive presence is a complex package of presence, appearance, body language and verbal language. When someone I'm working with is described as lacking executive presence, the first place I always look is at their language.

Our Habits Can Hurt Us

Reo, a leader I was coaching, was hoping to be promoted into the C-suite later that year. His performance was exemplary, and he had the figures to back up his achievements. Yet there was one issue that kept getting raised by his leadership team, and that was his perceived lack of executive presence. He was a tremendously intelligent, highly analytical, and fairly quiet and humble man who projected a calm and rational energy that served him well as an executive. Clients appreciated his steady explanatory manner of presenting, so it wasn't his style that posed a barrier to his effectiveness – it was his language.

After observing Reo present to his team one day, it struck me how much "qualifying" language he used. I define qualifying language as language that highlights a person's lack of confidence. This includes words that imply uncertainty (e.g., "like," "perhaps," "might," "guess" and "maybe") as opposed to definitive words (e.g., "will," "can" and "must"). In the span of a 10-minute conversation with Reo, I noted that he used the word "perhaps" exactly 12 times (yes, I counted). This was clearly a nervous verbal tic that had turned into a bad habit over time, because it made him appear as if he was never 100% sure of what he was doing.

We don't consciously register the actual words we hear when other people speak. It's important to realize that the impression we take away from someone's language is largely based on our own experiences, memories and biases. The language we use (particularly the way we talk about ourselves) tells a story to others. For that reason, we must be intentional in our word choices. Once Reo became aware of his verbal tic, he began to make a conscious effort to change his qualifying language and use more powerful words. In communication, self-awareness is key. Once Reo began to hear himself saying the words and understand just how insecure they made him sound as a leader, he was able to make a change very quickly. The first key step is to *notice*.

Practising Language: Helpful Tips

Know what you are saying about yourself and others. You want the narrative you are telling others, and yourself, to be a positive one. This equally applies to coaches as much as it does to those they are coaching. It's like a self-fulfilling prophecy. If you constantly tell people that you are tired and stressed, the chances of you being anything else are slim. When people ask you how you are and your standard answer is always "I'm so busy," you are sending a message to both yourself and those you are speaking to that you don't have time for them. Busy is a lonely place to be: it's a very closed state of mind. If you are not entirely sure what's coming out of your mouth, ask others. They will have a very good idea.

Use visual aids. One of the best ways of changing habits or chronic behaviour is through visual cues. Just like actors need cue cards to remember their lines, we too need constant reminders when we are practising a new skill or developing a new habit. Remember, this technique works for all the tools discussed in this book, not just language. Choose a sticker that represents the habit you are trying to change. For example, if you want

Know what you are
saying about yourself
and others.

to become a more attentive listener, a photo of a mouth with duct tape over it can be an effective reminder to do less talking and more listening. Stop signs could be used as cues to stop a behaviour, unicorns as cues to be nicer to people – there is a sticker out there with your name on it. Place these cues on your phone or anywhere else that is visually accessible to you throughout the day in order to remind you of what you want to practise.

Be intentional with the words you choose. Prepare important conversations ahead of time, and imagine how your words might "land" on someone.

Be mindful of your body language. If your physical stance is not aligned with the words you are speaking, you compromise the sincerity of your message. People will sense misalignment somewhere, and that can make them suspicious and mistrustful of your words. Whether your message is happy, sad, serious or exciting, make sure

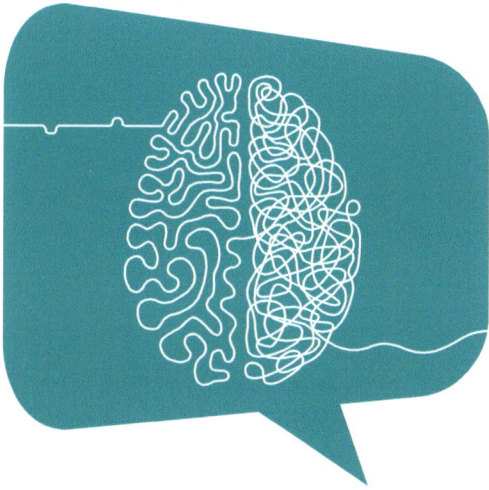

Busy is a lonely place
to be: it's a very closed
state of mind.

your body language aligns with your message. And remember, rolling your eyes doesn't only mean you are fed up: it's also a physical sign of contempt. So, pay close attention to what you might be inadvertently expressing.

Think in stop signs. To stop using the words "but" and "however," keep your sentences short. Stop trying to connect multiple sentences. Visualize a stop sign at the end of each thought. Pause. Give gravitas, or "weight," to your words. When communicating, taking your time and pausing when needed will not only make your message clearer, it will also add to your executive presence and give you an aura of confidence.

Giving
Feedback

This wouldn't be a book about coaching in organizations if it didn't address the elephant in the room: giving feedback. It still surprises me how much people struggle with this issue. Our inner need for approval and our desire to be liked and not to be "the bad guy" seem to far outweigh our ability to help others develop. It is essential to spend time with your team and create an environment where you and your team feel safe to share their observations and thoughts freely. This will prove to be far more valuable than simply keeping quiet until the annual performance review, all the while letting the underlying resentment build up around unaddressed issues and behaviours.

I have yet to come across an organization that has succeeded in making employees feel comfortable in, and be effective at, giving and receiving feedback. We meander down the garden path, take a tour around the issue and often end up in a vague place of polite confusion, incapable of articulating that one sentence that could help the other person be more successful.

Direct communication
has somehow
become equated with
abrasiveness, and that is
far from the truth.

Giving someone feedback does not equate to being mean. These do not need to be perceived as negative conversations, yet we have a tendency to turn them into moments fraught with emotional angst due to all of the baggage (ours, not the other person's) that we bring to the scene. If our intent is truly to help someone develop, to gain self-awareness around the impact they are having on the organization and to better understand how others see them, then we must conduct these conversations with clarity, curiosity and compassion. No more dancing around the issue in an attempt to avoid making people feel bad. Direct communication has somehow become equated with abrasiveness, and that is far from the truth. When carried out with understanding and empathy, a direct, honest conversation with an individual (even one about that individual's shortcomings) can have lasting positive consequences.

Trust that people understand they are not perfect and are generally capable of accepting constructive feedback. On an intellectual level, we all recognize that there is room for improvement in all aspects of our lives. By avoiding these conversations, you are choosing to treat those around you as if they were incapable, essentially writing them off. Remember that that is not your judgment to make. Own your behaviour and allow others around you to own theirs. If you truly feel that you can't be frank with someone on your team, you will never fully be able to set them up for success. Instead of avoiding honest communication to spare a person's feelings, perhaps you should consider whether that individual should even be a part of your team.

Begin creating dialogues, not downloads. A download is a conversation where you talk 100% of the time, downloading all your thoughts to someone else without giving them the opportunity to join in or respond. It's important to be curious about those around you and not be afraid to ask questions. When there is an opportunity for development, explore the issue together. Know where you draw the line regarding unacceptable behaviour, and address any issues immediately. Organizations often lose good employees because they fail to quickly and efficiently deal with ineffective leaders / team members who consistently make a negative impact. You know who they are, so do something about them.

Avoidance Disaster

A few years ago, I was asked to coach a young woman named Maja, who was an up-and-coming manager considered to be a top performer in her organization. The external customers loved her. She was bright, creative and driven. As a result, she generated a lot of revenue for the business. Yet within the four walls of her office, her dysfunctional behaviour surfaced. While Maja considered her customers to be esteemed and worthy of her time, she did not grant the same status to her colleagues and repeatedly demonstrated as such through her words and actions. Despite her unacceptable behaviour behind closed office doors, Maja was fully expecting to be promoted later that year based on her stellar performance and revenue generation.

Maja's manager, Jacob (the regional VP), acted like the benevolent uncle of the office. He enjoyed being seen as a kind, wise mentor to the staff. He avoided conflict, rarely held people accountable and allowed the "power" culture of some individuals to grow without boundaries. I spoke with Jacob about setting clear boundaries for Maja's behaviour and giving her long overdue feedback concerning her ill treatment of other employees. She was constantly starting rumours about her colleagues, dictating to whom her team members should and should not speak, and stirring the drama pot every chance she got. Jacob's response was that Maja just needed time to mature. After all, she was his star player, and all the customers loved her. What if she didn't appreciate his "hard" feedback and decided to take her skills elsewhere? Unfortunately, so long as management continued to avoid having the much-needed development conversations required for Maja to take accountability for her behaviour, external coaching was doomed to fail.

Approximately two weeks later, Jacob finally decided to have a conversation with Maja. Unfortunately, he decided to apply the often misleading "sandwich" method of delivering feedback. He began with a positive message, acknowledging all of Maja's efforts and highlighting how happy he was with her client work. Then he moved on to constructive feedback, telling her she needed to pay more attention to the impact she was having on her team and to be more respectful to her colleagues. He ended the conversation with the verbal equivalent of a high-five, concentrating once again on all the incredible work she had achieved.

Shortly after, Jacob informed Maja that she had been passed up for promotion and that it was given to one of her colleagues instead. Maja was obviously confused about how this could have happened when he'd recently finished telling her about her stellar performance in the organization. Jacob explained that there were two candidates and only one position, so a choice had to be made. So, Maja missed out on a huge development opportunity largely due to Jacob's lack of leadership and courage. By choosing to misguide her with ambiguous feedback rather than being crystal clear in his message and working with her to correct her behaviour, he ultimately harmed her. This type of feedback conversation is unfortunately very common in organizations, and it only creates confusion and mistrust within employees. It does not draw a clear line between acceptable and unacceptable behaviour, it does not probe the motivating factors behind an individual's behaviour and it certainly does not develop a case for change.

One year later, Maja's offensive behaviour had escalated to the point where she was fired. During her six years at the organization, she was directly responsible for at least six individuals quitting, not to mention the tsunami of misery and drama she created amongst other members of her team. With stronger leadership and more direct feedback conversations, would she have been able to develop her own leadership skills and sense of personal accountability? Perhaps. Unfortunately, we will never know.

Practising Feedback: Helpful Tips

Start with clear expectations of both responsibilities and behaviours. "Excellence" is a highly subjective term. Help people understand what you are hoping to achieve and how they can contribute to that goal. If you have templates or examples, share them. If people need more development or training to thrive in their roles, make it happen. Do your absolute best to set them up for success.

Be clear and concise. When it comes to feedback conversations, skirting around the issue, allowing too much initial chit chat and babbling for too long only serve to increase anxiety all around. Feedback conversations are often viewed by our brains as threatening. So, while most people can readily receive constructive feedback, it may take time for them to fully process and accept the information. The more frequently and directly you have these conversations, the less threatening they become.

Use facts, not judgments. It is so easy to sprinkle our biases into feedback conversations that we often don't even realize we are doing it. Statements like, "You're not a team player," or, "You seem to be disengaged," are not facts. On the other hand, statements like, "I noticed that you didn't attend the last three team events," or "I saw that you missed yesterday's deadline" are facts. Only undisputable, objective facts can pave the way for the most effective feedback conversations.

Follow factual observations with a question. For example, "Are you ok?" is a great question to ask, especially if an individual's behaviour is not consistent with their usual pattern. We are often not aware of what's happening in employees' lives outside of the office, so it's important to be curious and dig deeper. It's the only way to truly understand the motivation behind an individual's behaviour. "Can you help me understand?" is another great question that invites the person to open up without judgement. Turn the feedback conversation into a real coaching dialogue.

Ask the person to suggest solutions. Avoid asking a question like, "What should *we* do about this?" and instead ask, "What do *you* want to do to change this?" followed by, "How can I support you in achieving this?" Pose the question in a way that lays the responsibility on the individual. Trying to soften the blow by sharing in the ownership only serves to take away optimal learning opportunities from that individual.

Be timely. Don't avoid having feedback conversations. Small issues can quickly turn into big ones, which will only make the conversation harder to have.

Separate positive and constructive feedback conversations. If a person has accomplished something great, acknowledge it on its own separate occasion. It shouldn't be the opening to a constructive feedback conversation. Recognize the person's achievement, and give them time to digest your positive feedback. People sometimes struggle with positive feedback, because they've learned it is often followed by constructive (or "negative") feedback. Take five minutes and tell someone how much you appreciate their hard work. Ask them to walk you through the steps that led them to succeed in a project or task. Finally, celebrate their success with them. If it's been some time since you had a positive feedback conversation with one of your team members, it's time to ask yourself why.

Encourage people to ask for feedback by doing so yourself. Normalize the sharing of observations and insights. Make it ok to fail as long as it's a learning process. Take feedback from a fearful conversation and turn it into an everyday, normal occurrence (an exercise many performance management systems discourage by limiting feedback conversations to specific times in the year through formal employee review processes). Avoid trying to make people feel wrong. Focus instead on helping people grow and develop.

Follow-up with people to help them stay on track. Before a feedback conversation ends, book a follow-up meeting with the individual. Give them enough time to try a few ideas and see what works in helping them change their behaviour. This scheduled check-in not only ensures that people remain accountable, it also gives you the opportunity to see where they are, how they are doing and whether there is anything further you can do to help them succeed. Great feedback conversations must have equally great follow-up conversations. After all, this is about a person's professional (and perhaps even personal) development. It's important, so make the time to help them see it through.

Final Words

My intention in writing this short book was two-fold:

1. I wanted to provide practical techniques and tools to help professionals (both leaders and team members) in organizations improve their communication by using coaching skills.

2. I wanted to, more importantly, challenge you to think about how you are showing up in life, at work, as a leader, as a colleague, as a parent, as a partner and as a human being.

It all boils down to changing your mindset to think like a coach in both your professional and personal life, starting with the following three steps:

1. Do the work.
2. Practise presence continuously.
3. Embrace the opportunity to grow (in both yourself and others).

This isn't easy work. It takes heightened awareness, strong dedication and a staunch willingness to change behaviours that may be posing obstacles in your life. In many situations and relationships, it will also take courage to achieve this.

As we often say in coaching, the only behaviour you can change is your own. Be honest with yourself. Identify where you can improve, then start taking steps to change – today! Small, incremental changes are key to sustainable behavioural change. Don't try to do too much at once. Pinpoint one or two things you want to practise, then start there. Practise them until they start to feel more natural. Eventually they will develop into new, positive habits.

The impact we have on others, particularly when we are in any kind of leadership role, is often much more influential than we think. Take ownership of your behaviour. Ask for feedback. Be open. And above all, pay attention *in* and to your life.

Acknowledgments

I would like to thank my clients and colleagues, who teach me something new every single day.

To my beta-readers Dave, Eric, Leonie, Paul and Robyn, thank you for validating that this could indeed be a book.

To my publishing team at CPA Canada, thank you for making this first book experience a positive one.

To Dana Tye Rally, a stalwart friend and an inspiring writing coach, thank you for your unwavering confidence in my abilities.

And to my husband Bruno, thank you for supporting every dream I have ever had since we met.

About the Author

Jennifer Gervès-Keen, MA, MCEC

Founder of JGK
Consulting, Jennifer
Gervès-Keen, MCEC,
is an award-winning
executive coach,
facilitator and
speaker who is known
for her direct, honest
approach (not to mention
her distinctive footwear). A passionate
life-long learner and a huge believer in the power
of words (on average finishing three-to-four
books every week), Jennifer is constantly pushing
her clients to read, listen and learn. Her innate
business acumen and her in-depth knowledge
of organizational dynamics coupled with her
international experience make her unique in the
coaching profession. A sought-after consultant

PHOTO CREDIT: Wendy McAlpine

and coach, Jennifer is committed to her clients' success and is truly seen as an enterprise-wide business partner who leaves a positive impact on the entirety of every organization she works with. Continually fascinated by humanity's forces and flaws, she views the world as a grand experiment and never gets bored with exploring the motivations behind human behaviour. When she is not travelling, you can find Jennifer on the west coast of Canada singing away to '80s songs in her Mini Cooper or enjoying time with her family and friends.